AAT

Bookkeeping Controls

Pocket Notes

These Pocket Notes support study for the following AAT qualifications:

AAT Foundation Certificate in Accounting – Level 2

AAT Foundation Diploma in Accounting and Business – Level 2

AAT Foundation Certificate in Bookkeeping – Level 2

AAT Foundation Award in Accounting Software – Level 2

AAT Level 2 Award in Accounting Skills to Run Your Business

AAT Foundation Certificate in Accounting at SCQF Level 5

Certificate: Accounting Technician (Level 3 AATSA)

British library cataloguing-in-publication data

A catalogue record for this book is available from the British Library.

Published by:
Kaplan Publishing UK
Unit 2 The Business Centre
Molly Millars Lane
Wokingham
Berkshire
RG41 2QZ

ISBN 978-1-78415-604-6

© Kaplan Financial Limited, 2016

Printed and bound in Great Britain.

KAPLAN PUBLISHI

CONTENTS

Preface

These Pocket Notes contain the key things that you need to know for the exam, presented in a unique visual way that makes revision easy and effective.

Written by experienced lecturers and authors, these Pocket Notes break down content into manageable chunks to maximise your concentration.

Quality and accuracy are of the utmost importance to us so if you spot an error in any of our products, please send an email to mykaplanreporting@kaplan.com with full details, or follow the link to the feedback form in MyKaplan.

Our Quality Co-ordinator will work with our technical team to verify the error and take action to ensure it is corrected in future editions.

A guide to the assessment

The assessment

BKCL is the second of two financial accounting assessments at Foundation Certificate in Accounting.

Bookkeeping Controls should not be taken prior to studying and taking Bookkeeping Transactions.

Examination

Bookkeeping Controls (BKCL) is assessed by means of a computer based assessment. The CBA will last for 2 hours and consist of 10 tasks.

In any one assessment, learners may not be assessed on all content, or on the full depth or breadth of a piece of content. The content assessed may change over time to ensure validity of assessment, but all assessment criteria will be tested over time.

Learning outcomes & weighting

1.	Understand payment methods	5%
2.	Understand controls in a bookkeeping system	5%
3.	Use control accounts	20%
4.	Use the journal	50%
5.	Reconcile a bank statement with the cash book	20%
Total		100%

Pass mark

To pass a unit assessment, students need to achieve a mark of 70% or more.

This unit contributes 16% of the total amount required for the Foundation Certificate in Accounting qualification.

1

Re-cap: Accounting for sales

- Sales day book.
- Sales returns day book.
- Posting the sales day book.
- Posting the sales returns day book.
- Cash receipts book.
- VAT.

The double entry bookkeeping for sales and receipts was studied within Bookkeeping Transaction

The basic entries are now built on for Bookkeeping Controls.

Sales day book

- list of invoices sent out to credit customers
- date
- invoice number
- customer name/account code
- invoice total analysed into net, VAT and total (gross)

- information copied from sales invoices
- before further processing must be totalled
- totals can be checked by cross casting £3,794.14 + £758.82 = £4,552.96

Sales Day book						
Date	Invoice No	Customer Name	Sales ledger code	Total (gross) £	VAT £	Net £
12/08/X3	69489	TJ Builder	SL21	2,004.12	334.02	1,670.10
12/08/X3	69490	McCarthy & Sons	SL08	1,485.74	247.62	1,238.12
12/08/X3	69491	Trevor Partner	SL10	1,063.10	177.18	885.92
				4,552.96	758.82	3,794.14

Analysed sales day book

Sometimes the net figure (actual sales) is analysed into different types of sale/product type.

Sales day book										
Date	Invoice No	Customer Name	Code	Total (gross) £	VAT £	Russia £	Poland £	Spain £	Germany £	France £
15/08/X1	167	Worldwide News	W5	3,000.00	500.00					2,500.00
	168	Local News	L1	240.00	40.00			200.00		
	169	The Press Today	P2	360.00	60.00				300.00	
	170	Home Call	H1	240.00	40.00			200.00		
	171	Tomorrow	T1	120.00	20.00					100.00
	172	Worldwide news	W5	3,600.00	600.00	3,000.00				
				7,560.00	1,260.00	3,000.00	–	400.00	300.00	2,600.00

Sales returns day book

- list of credit notes sent out to credit customers
- date
- credit note number
- customer name/account code
- credit note total analysed into net, VAT and total
- information copied from credit note.

SALES RETURNS DAY BOOK						
Date	Credit Note No.	Customer Name	Code	Total (gross) £	VAT £	Net £
28/08/X3	03561	Trevor Partner	SL10	125.48	20.91	104.57
28/08/X3	03562	TJ Builder	SL21	151.74	25.29	126.45
				277.22	46.20	231.02

As the sales day book can be analysed into different types of sales or products, so can the sales returns day book.

Posting the sales day book

General ledger

- at the end of each day/week/month SDB is totalled
- totals must then be posted to accounts in the general ledger.

Double entry:

Debit	Sales ledger control account	Total (gross) figure
Credit	Sales account	Net figure
Credit	VAT account	VAT amount

SALES DAY BOOK

Date	Invoice No	Customer Name	Sales ledger code	Total (gross) £	VAT £	Net £
12/08/X3	69489	TJ Builder	SL21	2,004.12	334.02	1,670.10
12/08/X3	69490	McCarthy & Sons	SL08	1,485.74	247.62	1,238.12
12/08/X3	69491	Trevor Partner	SL10	1,063.10	177.18	885.92
				4,552.96	758.82	3,794.14
				SLCA	VAT A/C	Sales A/C

Sales ledger control account

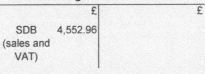

£		£
SDB (sales and VAT) 4,552.96		

Sales account

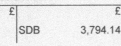

£		£
	SDB	3,794.14

VAT

£		£
	SDB	758.82

Subsidiary (sales) ledger

- sales ledger control account records the amount owing by all of the business's credit customers in total
- the business also needs to know how much each individual receivable owes - a ledger account is kept for each individual customer in a subsidiary ledger, the subsidiary (sales) ledger

Subsidiary (sales) ledger

Customer A

£		£

Customer B

£		£

Customer C

£		£

Posting to the subsidiary (sales) ledger

- each individual entry from the sales day book must be entered into the relevant customer account in the subsidiary (sales) ledger
- amount entered is the gross invoice total (including VAT)
- entered on the debit side of the account indicating that this is the amount the receivable owes.

Example

Now we return to the sales day book from earlier and post the individual entries to the subsidiary (sales) ledger.

TJ Builder		
	£	£
SDB	2,004.12	

McCarthy & Sons		
	£	£
SDB	1,485.74	

Trevor Partner		
	£	£
SDB	1,063.10	

Posting the sales returns day book

- as with the SDB the SRDB must also be posted to the general ledger accounts and subsidiary (sales) ledger accounts.

General ledger

Double entry:

Debit	Sales returns account	Net figure
Debit	VAT account	VAT total
Credit	Sales ledger control account	Total (gross) figure

Sales ledger control account

	£		£
SDB	4,552.96	SRDB	277.22

Sales account

	£		£
		SDB	3,794.14

VAT account

	£		£
SRDB	46.20	SDB	758.82

Sales returns account

	£		£
SRDB	231.02		

Subsidiary (sales) ledger

Each individual credit note must be entered in the customer's account:

- gross credit note total
- credit individual receivable account (reducing the amount owed).

CBA focus

For the examination you must know how th sales day book/sales returns day book is posted to the general ledger.

T J Builder

	£		£
SDB	2,004.12	SRDB	151.74

McCarthy & Sons

	£		£
SDB	1,485.74		

Trevor Partner

	£		£
SDB	1,063.10	SRDB	125.48

Cash receipts book

The cash receipts book records all money received into the business bank account. The CRB is analysed into columns as shown below.

The discount column is a memorandum column that shows what discount has been allowed to the customers for reasons such as an early settlement.

Cash receipts book						
Date	Narrative	Total £	VAT £	Receivables £	Cash sales £	Sundry £
3 Jul	A Brown	20.54	3.42		17.12	
5 Jul	S Smith & Co Ltd	9.30		9.30		
	P Priest	60.80		60.80		
	James & Jeans	39.02	6.50		32.52	
	LS Moore	17.00		17.00		
6 Jul	L White Ltd	5.16		5.16		
7 Jul	M N Furnishers Ltd	112.58				112.58
	R B Roberts	23.65		23.65		
	Light and Shade	86.95		86.95		
		375.00	9.92	202.86	49.64	112.58

- Date of receipt
- Details of receipt
- Total of receipts
- Total VAT on cash sales (the VAT on credit sales has been dealt with in the SDB)
- Total receipts from receivables
- Total net cash sales amount received
- Total receipts from sundry income

- entries to the cash receipts book come from either the remittance list or a photocopy of the paying in slip
- to check the totalling the cross casts should be checked:

	£
VAT	9.92
Receivables	202.86
Cash sales	49.64
Sundry income	112.58
Total	375.00

CBA focus

You will not be producing a cash book in th BKCL but it is important that you understar the cash book for bank reconciliation task.

VAT

- VAT is only ever recorded in the cash receipts book on cash sales or other income.

- VAT chargeable on credit sales is recorded in the sales day book. The "receipts from receivables" column of the CRB simply details the amount of money the receivable is paying off their account.

2

Re-cap: Accounting for purchases

- Purchases day book.
- Purchases returns day book.
- Posting the purchases day book.
- Posting the purchases returns day book.
- Cash payments book.
- VAT.

Purchases day book

- list of invoices received from credit suppliers
- date
- purchase invoice number (often internal consecutive number allocated)
- supplier name/account code

- invoice total analysed into net, VAT and total (gross)
- information copied from purchase invoice before further processing must be totalled
- totals can be checked by cross casting £663.89 + £132.77 = £796.66.

PURCHASES DAY BOOK						
Date	Invoice No.	code	supplier	Total £	VAT £	Net £
20X1						
7 May	2814	PL06	J Taylor	190.40	31.73	158.67
8 May	2815	PL13	McMinn Partners	288.14	48.02	240.12
	2816	PL27	D B Bros	96.54	16.09	80.45
9 May	2817	PL03	J S Ltd	221.58	36.93	184.65
				796.66	132.77	663.89

Analysed purchase day book

Sometimes the net figure (actual purchases)
is analysed into different types of purchase/
product type.

			PURCHASES DAY BOOK						
Date	Invoice no	Code	Supplier	Total	VAT £	01 £	02 £	03 £	04 £
05/02/X5	1161	053	Calderwood & Co	20.16	3.36	16.80			
05/02/X5	1162	259	Mellor & Cross	112.86	18.81		94.05		
05/02/X5	1163	360	Thompson Bros Ltd	42.86	7.14	35.72			

Purchases returns day book

- list of credit notes received from credit suppliers
- date
- credit note number (often internal consecutive number allocated)
- customer name/account code
- credit note total analysed into net, VAT and total
- information copied from credit note.

PURCHASES RETURNS DAY BOOK						
Date	Credit note no	Supplier	Code	Total (gross) £	VAT £	Net £
09/05/X1	02456	McMinn Partners	PL13	64.80	10.80	54.00
09/05/X1	02457	J S Ltd	PL03	72.00	12.00	60.00
				136.80	22.80	114.00

As the purchases day book can be analysed into different types of purchases or product types, the purchases returns day book can be analysed in the same way.

Posting the purchases day book (PDB)

General ledger

- at the end of each day/week/month PDB is totalled
- totals must then be posted to accounts in the general ledger.

Double entry:

Debit	Purchases account	Net figure
Debit	VAT account	VAT amount
Credit	Purchases ledger control account	Total (gross) figure

PURCHASES DAY BOOK

Date	Invoice No.	Code	Supplier	Total (gross) £	VAT £	Net £
20X1						
7 May	2814	PL06	J Taylor	190.40	31.73	158.67
8 May	2815	PL13	McMinn Partners	288.14	48.02	240.12
	2816	PL27	D B Bros	96.54	16.09	80.45
9 May	2817	PL03	J S Ltd	221.58	36.93	184.65
				796.66	132.77	663.89

Purchases account

	£		£
PDB	663.89		

Purchases ledger control account

	£		£
		PDB	796.66

VAT account

	£		£
PDB	132.77		

Subsidiary purchases ledger

- purchases ledger control account records the amount owing to all of the business's credit suppliers in total
- but also need information about each individual credit supplier's balance
- therefore ledger account kept for each individual supplier in a subsidiary ledger, the subsidiary (purchases) ledger.

Subsidiary (Purchases) Ledger

Supplier A

£	£

Supplier B

£	£

Supplier C

£	£

Posting to the subsidiary (purchases) ledger

- each individual entry from the purchases day book must be entered into the relevant supplier account in the subsidiary (purchases) ledger
- amount entered is the gross invoice total (including VAT)
- entered on the credit side of the account indicating that this is the amount owed to the supplier.

Example continued

Now we return to the purchases day book from earlier and post the individual entries to the subsidiary (purchases) ledger.

J Taylor		
£		£
	PDB	190.4

McMinn Partners		
£		£
	PDB	288.14

D B Bros		
£		£
	PDB	96.54

J S Ltd		
£		£
	PDB	221.58

Posting the purchases returns day book (PRDB)

- as with the PDB the PRDB must also be posted to the general ledger accounts and subsidiary (purchases) ledger accounts.

General ledger

Double entry:

Debit	Purchases ledger control account	Total (gross) figure
Credit	Purchases returns account	Net figure
Credit	VAT account	VAT total

Purchase account

	£		£
PRDB	663.89		

VAT account

	£		£
PRDB	132.77	PRDB	22.80

Purchase ledger control account

	£		£
PRDB	136.80	PDB	796.66

Purchases returns account

	£		£
		PRDB	114.00

Subsidiary (purchases) ledger

Each individual credit note must be entered in the supplier's account:

- gross credit note total
- debit individual supplier account (reducing the amount owing).

J Taylor			
	£		£
		PDB	190.4

McMinn Partners			
	£		£
PRDB	64.80	PDB	288.14

D B Bros			
	£		£
		PDB	96.54

J S Ltd			
	£		£
PRDB	72.00	PDB	221.58

Cash payments book

The cash payments book records all money paid out of the business bank account for whatever reason.

Date	Details	Cheque No	Total £	VAT £	Purchase ledger £	Cash £	Postage £
14/2	K Ellis	1152	80.00		80.00		
15/2	Hutt Ltd	1153	120.00	20.00		100.00	
16/2	Biggs Ltd	1154	200.00				200.00
			400.00	20.00	80.00	100.00	200.00

- Date of payment
- Details of payment
- Total of payment
- Total VAT on cash purchases
- Total payment to payables
- Total net cash purchases
- Total payment for post

- entries to the cash payments book come from either the cheque stubs or other banking documentation (see later chapter)
- to check the totalling the cross casts should be checked:

	£
VAT	20.00
Purchase ledger	80.00
Cash purchases	100.00
Postage	200.00
Total	400.00

VAT

- VAT is only ever recorded in the cash payments book on cash purchases or other payments for expenditure that attracts VAT that have not been entered in the purchases day book.
- any VAT on purchases on credit (i.e. payments to payables) has already been recorded in the purchases day book and posted to the ledger accounts from there

3

Re-cap: Ledger accounts and the trial balance

- Balancing ledger accounts.
- Opening balances.

Balancing the ledger accounts

In the examination you must know how to balance ledger accounts and do so with the appropriate narratives. It is these balances that then appear within a trial balance.

Let's review how to balance off a ledger account.

Example

Here is a typical cash (or bank) account:

Cash account

	£		£
Capital	10,000	Purchases	3,000
Sales	4,000	Rent	500
Receivables	5,000	Payables	1,500

Step 1	Total both debit and credit side and make a note of the totals.
Step 2	Insert higher of totals as total for both sides (leaving a line before inserting totals).

Cash account

	£		£
Capital	10,000	Purchases	3,000
Sales	4,000	Rent	500
Receivables	5,000	Payables	1,500
	———		———
	19,000		19,000
	———		———

Step 3 On the side with the smaller total, insert the figure (£14,000) which makes it add up to the overall total (£19,000) and call this the balance carried down (balance c/d).

Cash account

	£		£
Capital	10,000	Purchases	3,000
Sales	4,000	Rent	500
Receivables	5,000	Payables	1,500
		Balance c/d	14,000
	19,000		19,000

Step 4 On the opposite side of the account, enter the same figure as the balance c/d (£14,000), below the total line. The narrative should be balance brought down (balance b/d).

Cash account

	£		£
Capital	10,000	Purchases	3,000
Sales	4,000	Rent	500
Receivables	5,000	Payables	1,500
		Balance c/d	14,000
	19,000		19,000
Balance b/d	14,000		

This shows that after all of these transactions there is £14,000 of cash left as an asset in the business (a debit balance = an asset).

CBA focus

In the CBA, you will probably have to select narratives from a drop-down menu. Ensure you review the options fully before making your selection. Be careful with the keyboard and mouse when entering in balances and selecting options! A slip of a finger can cost you marks!

Debit and credit balances

- balance brought down on debit side is a debit balance and represents either an expense, an asset or drawings.
- balance brought down on credit side is a credit balance and represents either income, a liability or capital.

Opening balances

If an opening balance is to be entered into ledger account then you must know if it is a debit or a credit balance.

Remembering the mnemonic DEAD CLIC helps to determine if an entry should be made on the debit side or the credit side of ledger account.

Rules

Debit balances	Credit balances
Expenses	Liabilities
Assets	Income
Drawings	Capital

Example

Opening balances are given as follows:

Sales	£51,000
Sales ledger control	£15,000
Electricity	£2,000
Purchase ledger control	£13,000

Enter these as opening balances in the ledger accounts.

Sales account

£		£
	Opening balance	51,000

Income – credit balance

Sales ledger control account

	£		£
Opening balance	15,000		

Asset – debit balance

Electricity account

	£		£
Opening balance	2,000		

Expense – debit balance

Purchases ledger control account

£		£
	Opening balance	13,000

Liability – credit balance

CBA focus

In the examination you will be required to enter opening balances in selected ledger accounts so learn these rules.

Sales and purchases returns

- sales returns – opposite to sales (income) therefore a debit balance
- purchases returns – opposite to purchases (expense) therefore a credit balance.

Discounts allowed and discounts received

- discounts allowed to customers – an expense therefore a debit balance
- discounts received from suppliers – opposite to discounts allowed (expense) therefore a credit balance.

The balances for returns and for discounts are not as obvious as some so make sure you understand the logic of which side the opening balance appears.

Subsidiary (sales) ledger balances

- receivables therefore assets therefore debit balances.

Subsidiary (purchases) ledger balances

- payables therefore liabilities therefore credit balances.

4

Errors and suspense accounts

- What is a trial balance?
- Errors.
- Journal entries.
- Suspense account.
- Correcting errors and clearing the suspense account.

What is a trial balance?

- list of all of the ledger balances in the general ledger
- debit balances and credit balances listed in separate columns
- the total of the debit balances should equal the total of the credit balances.

Example

Trial balance

	Debit balances £	Credit balances £
Sales		5,000
Wages	100	
Purchases	3,000	
Rent	200	
Car	3,000	
Receivables	100	
Payables		1,400
	6,400	6,400

Debit or credit balance?

If you are just given a list of balances you must know whether they are debit or credit balances.

Remember the rules!

Debit balances	Credit balances
Asset	Liability
Expense	Income
Drawings	Capital

Errors

In a manual accounting system errors will be made – some are identified by extracting a trial balance but others are not.

Errors not identified by extracting a trial balance

Errors of original entry
error made when transaction first entered into primary records

Errors of principle
entry made in fundamentally wrong type of account i.e. revenue expense entered into capital/non-current asset account

Errors of omission
a transaction is not entered at all in the primary records

Errors of commission
entry made in wrong account although account of the correct type ie. rent expense entered into electricity expense account

Compensation errors
two or more errors which are exactly equal and opposite

Single entry
only one side of an entry made

Casting error
account incorrectly balanced

Errors identified by extracting a trial balance

Transposition error
numbers transposed in recording i.e. 98 shown as 89

Extraction error
account balance entered on trial balance as wrong figure

Did you know? A transposition error can be identified by the difference being exactly divisible by 9!

Journal entries

- written instruction to bookkeeper to put through a double entry which has not been sourced from the books of prime entry
- used for correction of errors/adjustments/ unusual items
- only used for adjusting double entry errors in the general ledger – not used for entries in the subsidiary (sales) or subsidiary (purchases) ledgers.

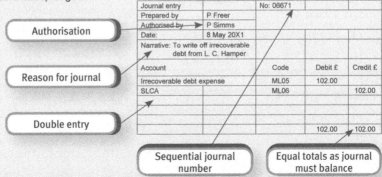

Authorisation

Reason for journal

Double entry

Journal entry		No: 06671		
Prepared by	P Freer			
Authorised by	P Simms			
Date:	8 May 20X1			
Narrative: To write off irrecoverable debt from L. C. Hamper				
Account		Code	Debit £	Credit £
Irrecoverable debt expense		ML05	102.00	
SLCA		ML06		102.00
			102.00	102.00

Sequential journal number

Equal totals as journal must balance

Suspense account

Used in two circumstances

- Bookkeeper does not know one side of an entry therefore posts it to a suspense account

  Example
  £200 received but bookkeeper does not know what it is for so debits cash receipts book and credits suspense account

- When trial balance totals disagree used to temporarily balance the trial balance

  Example
  Total of debit balances on trial balance is £35,000 but total of credit balances is £34,000. 1,000 credited to suspense account to make trial balance totals equal

Correcting errors and clearing the suspense account

- errors corrected by putting through a journal for the correcting entry.

How to find correcting entry

- work out the double entry that has been done
- work out the double entry that should have been done
- draft journal entry to go from what has been done to what should have been done.

CBA focus

In the examination have these 3 questions to mind..

(1) What has been done?

(2) What should have been done?

(3) How do we correct it?

Example

journal entries

(i) An amount of £200 for electricity bill payments was entered into the rent account.

What has been done?

| Debit | Rent account | £200 |
| Credit | Bank account | £200 |

What should have been done?

| Debit | Electricity account | £200 |
| Credit | Bank account | £200 |

How do we correct it? – Journal entry

| Debit | Electricity account | £200 |
| Credit | Rent account | £200 |

(ii) A purchase invoice for £1,000 had not been entered into the books of prime entry (VAT).

What has been done?

No entries at all

What should have been done?

| Debit | Purchases account | £1,000 |
| Credit | Purchases ledger control account | £1,000 |

How do we correct it? – Journal entry

| Debit | Purchases account | £1,000 |
| Credit | Purchases ledger control account | £1,000 |

(iii) An irrecoverable debt for £100 is to be written off.

This is not correction of an error but an adjustment to be made.

Journal entry

Debit	Irrecoverable debt expense account	£100
Credit	Sales ledger control account	£100

(iv) A contra entry for £500 has been entered in the general ledger control accounts but has not been entered in the subsidiary (purchases) ledger.

No journal entry is required as the error is not in the general ledger but the subsidiary ledger. However the payable's account in the subsidiary (purchases) ledger must be debited to reflect this contra entry.

CBA focus

In most examinations you will be required to draft journal entries to correct errors.

Errors and the suspense account

Some errors made will affect the trial balance and therefore are part of the suspense account balance.

Example

(i) Discounts allowed of £150 have been entered as a credit entry in the discounts allowed account

What has been done?

Credit	Discounts allowed account	£150
Credit	Sales ledger control account	£150

What should have been done?

Debit	Discounts allowed account	£150
Credit	Sales ledger control account	£150

How do we correct it? – Journal entry

Debit	Discounts allowed account	£300
Credit	Suspense account	£300

The discounts allowed account has been credited rather than debited with £150 therefore to turn this into a debit of £150 it needs to be debited with £300. No other account is incorrect so the other side of the entry is to the suspense.

(ii) The balance for motor expenses of £400 has been omitted from the trial balance.

What has been done?

The motor expenses balance of £400 has been omitted from the trial balance.

What should be done?

A £400 debit balance (expense) must appear on the trial balance.

How do we correct it? – Journal entry

Debit   Motor expenses (TB)   £400
Credit Suspense account   £400

Clearing the suspense account

The suspense account cannot remain as a permanent account and must eventually be investigated and cleared.

Example

A business has a suspense account with a debit balance of £80.

The following errors were noted:

(i) rent of £750 was entered into the rent account as £570

(ii) an advertising bill of was overstated in the advertising account by £100

Journals

(i)	Debit	Rent account	£180
	Credit	Suspense account	£180
(ii)	Debit	Suspense account	£100
	Credit	Advertising account	£100

Suspense account			
	£		£
Opening balance	80		
Advertising	100	Rent	180
	180		180

The suspense account is now cleared.

CBA focus

In most examinations you will be required to draft journal entries to clear a suspense account balance but usually there are only two adjustments required to be made to clear the balance.

chapter

5

Control account reconciliations

- Sales ledger control account.
- Sales ledger control account reconciliation.
- Purchases ledger control account.
- Purchases ledger control account reconciliation.
- VAT control accounts.

Sales ledger control account

- total receivables account
- sales invoices posted from sales day book
- credit notes posted from sales returns day book
- receipts from customers posted from cash receipts book.

Example

writing up the sales ledger control account the opening balance at 1 May on the sales ledger control account is £3,400.

Sales ledger control account

	£		£
Opening balance	3,400		

Asset – debit balance

- total from sales day book for month of May £20,600

Sales ledger control account

	£		£
Opening balance	3,400		
SDB	20,600		

Full double entry:

Debit   Sales ledger control account

Credit   Sales and VAT accounts

- total from sales returns day book for month of May £1,800

Sales ledger control account

	£		£
Opening balance	3,400	SRDB	1,800
SDB	20,600		

Full double entry:

Debit   Sales returns and VAT accounts

Credit   Sales ledger control account

- total from receivables column in cash receipts book of £19,500

Sales ledger control account

	£		£
Opening balance	3,400	SRDB	1,800
SDB	20,600	CRB	19,500

Full double entry:

Debit   Cash book

Credit   Sales ledger control account

- total of discounts allowed column in Discounts allowed book [DAB] £1,200.

Sales ledger control account

	£		£
Opening balance	3,400	SRDB	1,800
SDB	20,600	CRB	19,500
		DAB	1,200

Full double entry:

Debit   Discounts allowed account

Credit   Sales ledger control account

Other entries to the sales ledger control account

There are two other potential entries in the sales ledger control account:

- irrecoverable debts written off – when a debt is highly unlikely to be received
- contra entry – when money is owed to a supplier who is also a customer and therefore owes money – the two amounts are set off against each other.

Example

Irrecoverable debts written off

- a customer owing £400 has gone into liquidation and therefore it has been decided to write this debt off as bad.

Sales ledger control account

	£		£
Opening balance	3,400	SRDB	1,800
SDB	20,600	CRB	19,500
		DAB	1,200
		Irrecoverable debt expense	400

Full double entry:

Debit   Irrecoverable debt expense account

Credit   Sales ledger control account

Example continued – contra entry

- a customer who owes us £200 is also a supplier and we owe him £300. It has been agreed that the two amounts should be set off by a contra entry leaving only £100 owed by us to the supplier.

Sales ledger control account

	£		£
Opening balance	3,400	SRDB	1,800
SDB	20,600	CRB	19,500
		DAB	1,200
		Irrecoverable debt write off	400
		Contra	200

Full double entry:

Debit   Purchases ledger control account

Credit Sales ledger control account

Example continued – balancing the sales ledger control account

Sales ledger control account

	£		£
Opening balance	3,400	SRDB	1,800
SDB	20,600	CRB	19,500
		DAB	1,200
		Irrecoverable debt write off	400
		Contra	200
		Balance c/d	900
	24,000		24,000
Balance b/d	900		

This shows that at the end of May we have total receivables of £900.

Sales ledger control account reconciliation

- the sales ledger control account is written up using totals from the sales day book, sales returns day book and cash receipts book

- individual accounts for receivables in the subsidiary (sales) ledger are written up using the individual entries from the sales day book, sales returns day book and cash receipts book

- as both are written up from the same sources of information, at the end of the period the balance on the sales ledger control account should equal the total of the list of balances in the subsidiary (sales) ledger.

SLCA balance	=	Total of list of subsidiary (sales) ledger

Purpose of sales ledger control account reconciliation

- to show that SLCA does in fact equal the total of the list of balances

- to indicate that there are errors in either the SLCA or the subsidiary (sales) ledger accounts if the two are not equal

- to find the correct figure for total receivables to appear in the trial balance.

Preparing a sales ledger control account reconciliation

Step 1

- Extract list of balances from subsidiary (sales) ledger accounts and total.

Step 2

- Balance the sales ledger control account.

Step 3

- If the two figures are different the reasons for the difference must be investigated.

Step 4

- correct any errors that affect the sales ledger control account
- find corrected balance on sales ledger control account.

Step 5

- correct any errors that affect the total of the list of balances from the subsidiary (sales) ledger
- find corrected total of list of subsidiary (sales) ledger balances.

Example

Sales ledger control account reconciliation

The balance on the sales ledger control account at 31 May is £4,100. The individual balances on the subsidiary (sales) ledger are as follows:

	£
Receivable A	1,200
Receivable B	300
Receivable C	2,000
Receivable D	1,000

Step 1

- Extract list of balances from subsidiary (sales) ledger accounts and total

	£
Receivable A	1,200
Receivable B	300
Receivable C	2,000
Receivable D	1,000
	4,500

Step 2

- Balance the sales ledger control account

The balance has been given as £4,100.

Step 3

- If the two figures are different the reasons for the difference must be investigated

You are given the following information:

- a page of the sales day book had been undercast by £100

- a credit note for £50 to Receivable A had been entered into A's subsidiary (sales) ledger account as an invoice

- a contra entry with Receivable B for £200 had only been entered in the sales ledger control account and not the individual subsidiary (sales) ledger account.

Step 4

- correct any errors that affect the sales ledger control account
- find corrected balance on sales ledger control account.

Sales ledger control account

	£		£
Original balance	4,100		
SDB undercast	100	Correct balance	4,200
CPB	4,200		4,200
Correct balance	4,200		

If the sales day book was undercast then the amount posted to the sales ledger control account was £100 too small and therefore an additional debit entry for £100 is needed in the control account.

The other two adjustments affect the individual accounts not the control account.

Step 5

- correct any errors that affect the total of the list of balances from the subsidiary (sales) ledger
- find corrected total of list of subsidiary (sales) ledger balances.

	£
Total list of balances	4,500
Less: Credit note entered as invoice	(100)
Less: Contra	(200)
Corrected list of balances	4,200

As the credit note for £50 had been entered as an invoice, the list of balances must be reduced by £100 to reflect the removal of the invoice and the entry of the credit note.

The contra had only been entered in the sales ledger control account therefore £200 must be deducted from the list of balances.

Credit balances on sales ledger accounts

- normally a receivable's balance on his subsidiary (sales) ledger account will be a debit balance brought down
- sometimes however balance will be a credit balance.

Reasons for credit balance:

Overpayment by receivable

Misposting to subsidiary (sales) ledger account

Treatment of credit balance

- when the list of subsidiary (sales) ledger balances is drawn up and totalled, the credit balance must be deducted rather than added.

Purchases ledger control account

- total payables account
- purchase invoices posted from purchases day book
- credit notes posted from purchases returns day book
- payments to suppliers posted from cash payments book
- discounts received from discounts received day book.

Example

Writing up the purchases ledger control account

- the opening balance at 1 May on the purchases ledger control account is £2,100

Purchases ledger control account

	£		£
		Opening balance	2,100

Liability - credit balance

- total from purchases day book for month of May £15,800

Purchases ledger control account

	£		£
		Opening balance	2,100
		PDB	15,800

Full double entry:

Debit   Purchases and VAT accounts

Credit   Purchases ledger control account

- total from purchases returns day book for month of May £900

Purchases ledger control account

	£		£
PRDB	900	Opening balance	2,100
		PDB	15,800

Full double entry:

Debit   Purchases ledger control account

Credit   Purchases returns and VAT accounts

- total from payables column in cash payments book of £13,000

Purchases ledger control account

	£		£
PRDB	900	Opening balance	2,100
CPB	13,000	PDB	15,800

Full double entry:

Debit Purchases ledger control account

Credit Cash Book

- total of discounts received column in discounts received book £700

Purchases ledger control account

	£		£
PRDB	900	Opening balance	2,100
CPB	13,000	PDB	15,800
DRB	700		

Full double entry:

Debit Purchases ledger control account

Credit Discounts received account

- a customer who owes us £200 is also a supplier and we owe him £300. It has been agreed that the two amounts should be set off by a contra entry leaving only £100 owed by us to the supplier.

Purchases ledger control account

	£		£
PRDB	900	Opening balance	2,100
CPB	13,000	PDB	15,800
DRB	700		
Contra	200		

Full double entry:

Debit Purchases ledger control account

Credit Sales ledger control account

Balancing the purchases ledger control account

Purchases ledger control account

	£		£
PRDB	900	Opening balance	2,100
CPB	13,000	PDB	15,800
DRB	700		
Contra	200		
Balance c/d	3,100		
	17,900		17,900
		Balance b/d	3,100

This shows that we have payables totalling £3,100 at the end of May.

CBA focus

In the examination you will have to know the accounting entries for both the sales ledger control account and the purchases ledger control account.

Purchases ledger control account reconciliation

- the purchases ledger control account is written up using totals from the purchases day book, purchases returns day book and cash payments book

- individual accounts for payables in the subsidiary (purchases) ledger are written up using the individual entries from the purchases day book, purchases returns day book and cash payments book

- as both are written up from the same sources of information then at the end of the period the balance on the purchases ledger control account should equal the total of the list of balances in the subsidiary (purchases) ledger.

PLCA balance = Total of list of subsidiary (purchases) ledger

Purpose of purchases ledger control account reconciliation

- to show that the PLCA does in fact equal the total of the list of balances

- to indicate that there are errors in either the PLCA or the subsidiary (purchases) ledger accounts if the two are not equal

- to find the correct figure for total payables to appear in the trial balance.

Preparing a purchases ledger control account reconciliation

Step 1

- Extract list of balances from subsidiary (purchases) ledger accounts and total.

Step 2

- Balance the purchases ledger control account.

Step 3

- If the two figures are different the reasons for the difference must be investigated.

Step 4

- correct any errors that affect the purchases ledger control account
- find corrected balance on the purchases ledger control account.

Step 5

- correct any errors that affect the total of the list of balances from the subsidiary (purchases) ledger
- find corrected total of list of subsidiary (purchases) ledger balances.

 e.g

Example

Purchases ledger control account reconciliation

The balance on the purchases ledger control account at 31 May is £2,000. The individual balances on the subsidiary (purchases) ledger are as follows:

	£
Payable E	800
Payable F	600
Payable G	400
Payable H	700

Step 1

- Extract list of balances from subsidiary (purchases) ledger accounts and total

	£
Payable E	800
Payable F	600
Payable G	400
Payable H	700
	2,500

Step 2

- Balance the purchases ledger control account

  The balance has been given as £2,000.

Step 3

- If the two figures are different the reasons for the difference must be investigated.

You are given the following information:

- a page of the purchases returns day book had been overcast by £1,000

- discounts received from suppliers totalling £680 had not been posted to the control account

- an invoice to payable G for £350 had been entered into the individual account in the subsidiary (purchases) ledger as £530.

Step 4

- correct any errors that affect the purchases ledger control account
- find corrected balance on purchases ledger control account.

Purchases ledger control account

	£		£
Discounts received	680	Original balance	2,000
Corrected balance	2,320	PRDB overcast	1,000
	3,000		3,000
		Corrected balance	2,320

If the purchases returns day book was overcast then the amount posted to the purchases ledger control account on the debit side for returns was £1,000 too big

and therefore an additional credit entry for £1,000 is needed in the control account.

The discounts received of £680 were omitted from the control account therefore the control account must be debited with this amount.

Step 5

- correct any errors that affect the total of the list of balances from the subsidiary (purchases) ledger
- find corrected total of list of subsidiary (purchases) ledger balances.

	£
Total list of balances	2,500
Less: transposition error on invoice (530 – 350)	(180)
Corrected total list of balances	2,320

The invoice had been entered as £180 higher than it should have been and therefore the total of the list of balances must reduced by £180.

Example

Sales ledger control account reconciliation

	£
Balance per sales ledger control account	4,580
Total of list of subsidiary (sales) ledger balances	4,780
Difference	200

In this case the list of balances is £200 higher than the control account total. What may have caused this?

Suppose that one balance in the list of balances is for £100. It is possible that this is in fact a credit balance of £100 but has been incorrectly added into the list of balances rather than being deducted.

Alternatively if the control account includes an irrecoverable debt write off of £200 then it is possible that this has not been entered into the individual account in the subsidiary (sales) ledger causing the subsidiary (sales) ledger balances to be higher than the control account balance.

CBA focus

In the examination you will always have to prepare a sales or purchases ledger control account reconciliation. The style of these questions is as follows:

(i) Write up the sales/purchases ledger control account.

(ii) Total the list of balances.

(iii) Compare the balance on the control account to the total list of balances and determine the difference.

(iv) Identify what the difference may have been caused by.

Look for numbers in the control account or list of balances which either equal the difference identified or is twice as much as the difference and this could be the cause of the difference.

VAT control accounts

As seen in Bookkeeping Transactions, as the sales, sales returns, purchases and purchases returns are entered into the accounts, the VAT is also calculated and accounted for.

Within the BKCL assessment you may be given extracts from the day books and asked to enter the relevant figures into the VAT control account, or you may be asked to list the entries required to the control account indicating whether they would be on the debit or credit side of the VAT control account.

It may also be a requirement to find the overall balance of the VAT control account i.e. to state what the balance is and whether it is owed to the tax authorities (HMRC) or whether a refund is due from them. The illustration above has shown us the VAT control account assuming that the balance brought down is on the credit side and therefore a liability. Although it is less likely, you may also encounter a VAT control account where the balance brought down is on the debit side and therefore an asset, meaning a refund is due to the business from the tax authorities.

VAT control account

	£		£
VAT on credit purchases		VAT on credit sales	
VAT on cash purchases		VAT on cash sales	
VAT on sales returns		VAT on purchases returns	
	___	Balance b/d	___
	___		___

Payroll procedures

- Gross pay and deductions.
- Total wages cost.
- Paying wages and salaries.
- Accounting for wages and salaries.
- Paying PAYE and NIC.

Gross pay and deductions

Gross pay

Made up of:

Basic wage + overtime + bonus + shift payment + commission etc

Net pay

	£
Gross pay	X
Less: PAYE	(X)
Less: Employee's NIC	(X)
Less: other deductions	(X)
Net pay to employee	X

PAYE

- deduction of income tax due on gross pay
- employer deducts correct amount of income tax for period from gross pay
- employer pays this income tax to HM Revenue and Customs (HMRC).

National Insurance Contributions (NIC)

- two types — employee's NIC
- — employer's NIC
- employee's NIC — deducted from gross pay by employer

  — paid over to HMRC by employer

- employer's NIC — additional payment to HMRC by employer.

Other possible deductions

- pension contributions
- payments under save as you earn scheme (SAYE)
- payments under give as you earn scheme (GAYE)
- others such as subscriptions to sports/social clubs, trade unions.

Total wages cost

Cost to employer = Gross pay + employer's NIC + employer's pension contributions

Paying wages and salaries

Cash
- very rare
- time-consuming
- security risk

Cheque
- time consuming
- only practical for small number of employees

Methods of paying wages and salaries

Bank giro credit
- transfer directly to employee's bank account

BACS
- most common method
- transactions recorded on magnetic tape/disc
- processed at BACS computer centre

Example

Gross pay of employee = £500 per week
PAYE = £100 for week
Employee's NIC = £80 for week
Employer's NIC = £90 for week

	£	
Gross pay	500	
Less: PAYE	(100)	Paid by employer to HMRC
Less: Employee's NIC	(80)	Paid by employer to HMRC
Employee's net pay	320	Paid to employee

Employer pays:

	£
Net pay to employee	320
PAYE to HMRC	100
Employee's NIC to HMRC	80
Employer's NIC to HMRC	90
Total cost to employer	590

Total wages cost to employer:

	£
Gross pay	500
Employer's NIC	90
	590

KAPLAN PUBLISHI

Accounting for wages and salaries

Double entry – two fundamentals

Can we change this to:
Cost to employer =
gross pay + employer's
NIC + employer's
pension contributions

PAYE and NIC
deductions paid over to
HMRC by employer

The wages and salaries control account is used
to ensure that all wages and salaries costs are
correctly paid out to the appropriate parties

Example

Double entry

Gross pay of employee	= £500 per week
PAYE	= £100 for week
Employee's NIC	= £80 for week
Employer's NIC	= £90 for week

Step 1 – Gross pay

Debit Wages expense account £590
Credit Wages and salaries control £590
          account

Wages expense account

	£		£
Wages and salaries control	590		

Wages and salaries control account

	£		£
		Wages expense	590

Step 2 – net pay

Debit	Wages and salaries control account (£500 – £100 – £80)	£320
Credit	Bank account	£320

Wages expense account

	£		£
Wages and salaries control	590		

Wages and salaries control account

	£		£
Bank	320	Wages expense	590

Step 3 – deductions payable to HMRC

Debit	Wages and salaries control account (£100 + £80)	£270
Credit	PAYE/NIC account	£270

Wages expense account

	£		£
Wages and salaries control	590		

Wages and salaries control account

	£		£
Bank	320	Wages expense	590
PAYE/NIC	270		

PAYE/NIC account

	£		£
		Wages and salaries control	270

Overall result – balance accounts

Wages expense account

	£		£
Wages and salaries control	590		
		balance c/d	590
	——		——
	590		590
	——		——
balance b/d	590		

= total wages cost for period (debit balance = expense)

Wages and salaries control account

	£		£
Bank	320	Wages expense	590
PAYE/NIC	270		
	——		——
	590		590
	——		——

= no balance – simply a control account.

PAYE/NIC

	£		£
Balance c/d	270	Wages and salaries control	270
	——		——
	270		270
	——		——
		Balance b/d	270

= amount due to HMRC
  (credit balance = liability).

CBA focus

The double entries are quite complicated but the key is to use the wages and salaries control account as it should be used, as a check that all costs have been appropriately accounted for.

Paying PAYE and NIC

- payment of amounts deducted and due for PAYE, employee's and employer's NIC made each month

- made by bank giro credit to HM Revenue and Customs

- one payment covering all employees.

Double entry

Debit	PAYE/NIC account
Credit	Bank account

PAYE/NIC account

	£		£
		Wages and salaries control	270
Balance c/d	270		
	270		270
Bank	270	Balance b/d	270

Bank reconciliations

- Calculating the balance on the cash book.
- Comparing cash book and the bank statement.
- Bank reconciliation statement.

Calculating the balance on the cash book

If a separate cash receipts book and separate cash payments book are used then the balance on the cash book at the end of the period is:

Balance on cash book = Opening cash book balance + Cash book receipts total − Cash book payments total

Example

A business had a balance on its cash book at 1 May of £750 debit. During May the cash receipts book shows a total of £5,340 and the cash payments book shows a total of £5,720.

Balance on cash book at end of May
= £750 + £5,340 − £5,720
= £370

CBA focus

Care must be taken if the opening balance on the cash book is a credit balance (overdraft balance).

Example

A business had a balance on its cash book at 1 May of £750 but this time it was a credit balance or overdraft balance. During May the cash receipts book shows a total of £5,340 and the cash payments book shows a total of £5,720.

Balance on cash book at end of May
= -£750 + £5,340 - £5,720
= £1,130 overdraft

Comparing the cash book and the bank statement

When the bank statement is received it should be checked to the cash book to ensure the accuracy of the cash book.

Debits and credits on bank statement

- a debit on the bank statement is a payment
- a credit on the bank statement is a deposit
- this is the opposite way round to the business ledger account as the bank statement is prepared from the bank's point of view.

Procedure

Step 1

- tick off items found in both cash book and on bank statement.

Step 2

- consider the unticked items in cash book and bank statement.

Unticked items in cash book

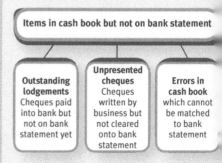

Items in cash book but not on bank statement

Outstanding lodgements
Cheques paid into bank but not on bank statement yet

Unpresented cheques
Cheques written by business but not cleared onto bank statement

Errors in cash book which cannot be matched to bank statement

CBA focus

The outstanding lodgements and unpresented cheques are both known as timing differences and are due to the operation of the bank clearing system. These will be the items you will need for the bank reconciliation statement. i.e. to prove that the bank statement and cash book balance agree with the exception of timing differences.

Unticked items on bank statement

Direct debits/ standing orders
payments made directly out of the bank which have not been entered into cash payments book

Direct credits/ BACS receipts
credits directly into the bank account which have not yet been entered into cash receipts book

Items on bank statement but not in cash book

Bank charges/ interest
not yet in cash book as cashier does not know about them until bank statement received

Errors in cash book
errors such as transposition errors which only come to light when cash book is compared to bank statement

Bank reconciliation statement

Step 1   Compare cash book to bank statement

- covered above.

Step 2   Enter items which are on bank statement but not yet in cash book into the cash book

- typical items include bank charges, direct debits, direct credits or standing orders

- correct any errors in the cash book.

Step 3   Balance amended cash book

- this should give the correct balance on the cash book

- this will not usually agree with the bank statement balance due to timing differences.

Step 4   Prepare bank reconciliation statement

Bank reconciliation statement

	£
Balance per bank statement	X
Less: unpresented cheques	(X
Add: outstanding lodgements	X
Balance per cash book	X

Once the unpresented cheques and outstanding lodgements have been taken into account the bank statement balance should agree to the amended cash book balance. The cash book and bank statement are reconciled.

Example

A company's cashier has compared the cash book for the month of May to the bank statement at 31 May. The following differences have been noted:

- bank charges on the bank statement not in cash book of £35
- direct debit of £100 on bank statement not in cash book
- cheques written by the business totalling £340 not yet on bank statement
- cheques paid into bank account totalling £200 not yet on bank statement.

The balance on the cash book before this reconciliation took place was a debit balance of £700 but the balance on the bank statement was £705 in credit.

Amend cash book

Cash book

	£		£
Original balance	700	Bank charges	35
		Direct debit	100
		Amended closing balance	565
	700		700
Amended cash book balance	565		

Prepare bank reconciliation statement

	£
Balance per bank statement	705
Less: unpresented cheques	(340)
Add: outstanding lodgements	200
Balance per cash book	565

The bank reconciliation should always be completed using a proforma like the one detailed below.

Although it is usual to see the proforma starting with the balance per bank statement, practice starting with the balance per updated cash book.

Balance per bank statement

Less:

Add:

Balance per updated cash book

Banking system

- Cheques.
- Clearing system.
- Other methods of receiving payment.
- Paying in slip.
- Bank statement.

Cheques

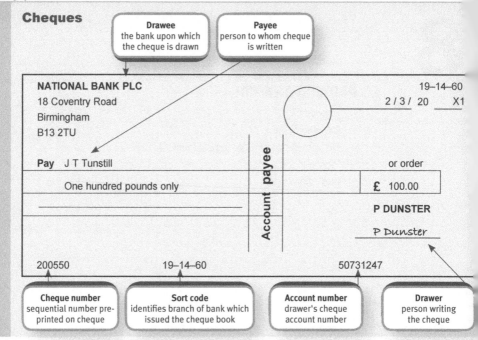

Drawee
the bank upon which the cheque is drawn

Payee
person to whom cheque is written

NATIONAL BANK PLC
18 Coventry Road
Birmingham
B13 2TU

19–14–60

2 / 3 / 20   X1

Pay J T Tunstill

Account payee

or order

One hundred pounds only

£ 100.00

P DUNSTER

P Dunster

200550

19–14–60

50731247

Cheque number
sequential number pre-printed on cheque

Sort code
identifies branch of bank which issued the cheque book

Account number
drawer's cheque account number

Drawer
person writing the cheque

Checks to make when receiving cheques

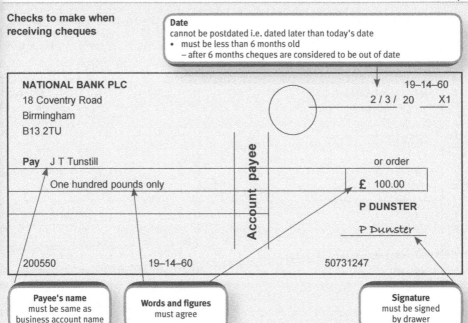

NATIONAL BANK PLC
18 Coventry Road
Birmingham
B13 2TU

19–14–60
2 / 3 / 20   X1

Pay J T Tunstill   or order

One hundred pounds only   **£** 100.00

                                    P DUNSTER

                                    P Dunster

Account payee

200550   19–14–60   50731247

Payee's name
must be same as business account name

Words and figures
must agree

Signature
must be signed by drawer

Cheque crossings

What is a crossing? Two vertical lines across cheque – usually with words

The 'account payee' crossing is the norma crossing on a pre-printed cheque – it mear the cheque can only be paid into the bank account of the payee.

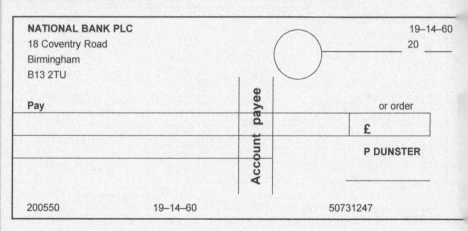

NATIONAL BANK PLC
18 Coventry Road
Birmingham
B13 2TU

19–14–60
20 _____

Pay

or order

£

P DUNSTER

Account payee

200550   19–14–60   50731247

Clearing system

All of the UK high street banks are involved in the clearing system which is a method by which the banks exchange cheques.

The relevance of the clearing system to these Units is that when cheques are paid into the bank account it will take three working days before the money is credited to the business bank account.

CBA focus

When preparing bank reconciliation statements you will find outstanding lodgements and unpresented cheques which are largely due to the time delay caused by the clearing system.

Other methods of receiving payment

Automated payments

Standing order
regular payments made directly into another bank account

Direct debit
allows the supplier to collect varying amounts from customer's bank account on a regular basis

Automated payments

Bank giro credit
regular payments made directly into another bank account

BACS
large amounts of transactions directly into bank accounts through the BACS computer centre – often used for wages and salaries payments

Credit card and debit cards

Credit card

- purchases made using credit card voucher/PIN
- credit card company pays supplier
- customer pays amounts due to credit card company on regular basis
- amount of purchase must not exceed retailer's floor limit without authorisation from credit card company
- credit card must be in date (start and expiry date)

Debit card

- purchase made using voucher/PIN
- money transferred directly from customer's bank account to supplier's bank account.

Paying in slip

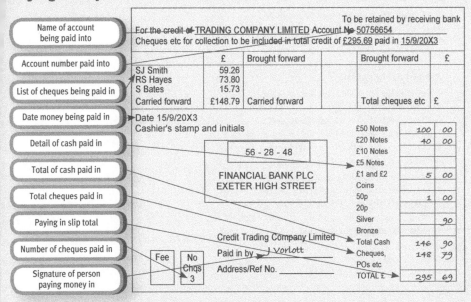

Name of account being paid into

Account number paid into

List of cheques being paid in

Date money being paid in

Detail of cash paid in

Total of cash paid in

Total cheques paid in

Paying in slip total

Number of cheques paid in

Signature of person paying money in

To be retained by receiving bank

For the credit of TRADING COMPANY LIMITED Account No 50756654
Cheques etc for collection to be included in total credit of £295.69 paid in 15/9/20X3

	£	Brought forward		Brought forward	£
SJ Smith	59.26				
RS Hayes	73.80				
S Bates	15.73				
Carried forward	£148.79	Carried forward		Total cheques etc	£

Date 15/9/20X3
Cashier's stamp and initials

56 - 28 - 48

FINANCIAL BANK PLC
EXETER HIGH STREET

Credit Trading Company Limited
Paid in by J Vorlott
Address/Ref No. _____

Fee | No Chqs 3

	£	
£50 Notes	100	00
£20 Notes	40	00
£10 Notes		
£5 Notes		
£1 and £2	5	00
Coins		
50p	1	00
20p		
Silver		90
Bronze		
Total Cash	146	90
Cheques, POs etc	148	79
TOTAL £	295	69

Electronic credit card sales

Most credit card sales nowadays are electronic using the PIN system therefore there is no need to pay anything into the bank.

Use of paying in slip

- before taking the cash/cheques/credit card vouchers/paying in slip to the bank it will normally be photocopied so that it can be used for entering the amounts paid in into the cash receipts book

- if the paying in slip is to be used to write up the cash receipts book then the amount of any settlement discount taken by any credit customers must be recorded together with the amount of the cheque received from them.

Bank statement

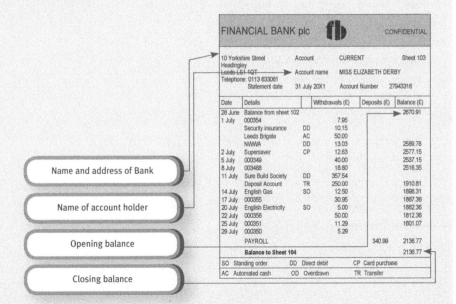

| FINANCIAL BANK plc | | | | CONFIDENTIAL |

10 Yorkshire Street
Headingley
Leeds LS1 1QT
Telephone: 0113 633061

Account   CURRENT   Sheet 103
Account name   MISS ELIZABETH DERBY
Statement date 31 July 20X1   Account Number 27943316

Date	Details		Withdrawals (£)	Deposits (£)	Balance (£)
28 June	Balance from sheet 102				2670.91
1 July	000354		7.95		
	Security insurance	DD	10.15		
	Leeds Brigate	AC	50.00		
	NWWA	DD	13.03		2589.78
2 July	Supersaver	CP	12.63		2577.15
5 July	000349		40.00		2537.15
8 July	003488		18.80		2518.35
11 July	Sure Build Society	DD	357.54		
	Deposit Account	TR	250.00		1910.81
14 July	English Gas	SO	12.50		1898.31
17 July	000355		30.95		1867.36
20 July	English Electricity	SO	5.00		1862.36
22 July	000356		50.00		1812.36
25 July	000351		11.29		1801.07
29 July	000350		5.29		
	PAYROLL			340.99	2136.77
	Balance to Sheet 104				2136.77

| SO | Standing order | DD | Direct debit | CP | Card purchase |
| AC | Automated cash | OD | Overdrawn | TR | Transfer |

Name and address of Bank

Name of account holder

Opening balance

Closing balance

Received periodically from the bank detailing payments and receipts from the account.

Terminology

When you have money in your bank account the bank says you are IN CREDIT.

When you have an overdraft the bank says you have a DEBIT BALANCE.

CBA focus

This terminology may seem to be opposite to that used in the ledger accounts but it is just that the bank statement is looking at the account balance in the bank's point of view. Therefore a debit balance in the business's ledger account means there is cash in the account and this will be called a credit balance by the bank (because the bank owes this to the business) and vice versa.

Index